JUN   2011

D0926457

From Fail to Win!
Learning from Bad Ideas

BUILDINGS and STRUCTURES

Nicola Barber

Chicago, Illinois

www.heinemannraintree.com
Visit our website to find out more information about Heinemann-Raintree books.

To order:
☎ Phone 888-454-2279
🖥 Visit www.heinemannraintree.com to browse our catalog and order online.

Edited by Andrew Farrow, Vaarunika Dharmapala, and Adrian Vigliano
Designed by Richard Parker
Original illustrations © Capstone Global Library Ltd 2011
Illustrated by Jeff Edwards
Picture research by Mica Brancic

Originated by Capstone Global Library Ltd
Printed and bound in China by South China Printing Company Ltd

14 13 12 11 10
10 9 8 7 6 5 4 3 2 1

Library of Congress Cataloging-in-Publication Data
Barber, Nicola.
  Buildings and Structures / Nicola Barber.
    p. cm.—(From Fail to Win)
  Includes bibliographical references and index.
  ISBN 978-1-4109-3907-4 (hardcover)
  1. Structural failures—Juvenile literature. I. Title.
  TA656.B37 2011
  624.1'71—dc22
  2010001459

Acknowledgments
The author and publisher are grateful to the following for permission to reproduce copyright material: Alamy pp. **14** (© guichaoua), **19** (© Peter Titmuss), **29** (© nagelestock.com); AP/Empics p. **41** (AP Photo/The News Tribune, Dean J. Koepfler); Corbis pp. **5** (© Bettmann), **11** (Reuters/© STR/Teruaki Ueno), **25** (© Bettmann), **26** (© Bettmann), **28** (Reuters/© Michaela Rehle), **31** (C. F. Murphy Associates/© G. E. Kidder Smith), **43** (© Bettmann), **46** (© Bettmann), **49** (© Bettmann); Getty Images pp. **7** (The Image Bank/joSon), **9** (AFP Photo DDP/David Hecker), **12** (Photodisc/Medioimages), **22** (Hulton Archive/Evening Standard), **30** (AFP Photo/Joe Klamar); PA pp. **18** (AP Photo/Jackie Green), **39** (AP Photo), **40** (AP Photo); Press Association Images p. **32** (AP/Pete Leabo); Rex Features p. **15** (Swani Gulshan); Santa Clarita Valley Historical Society p. **45**; Shutterstock p. **42** (Christopher Walker).

Cover photograph of the Tacoma Narrows Bridge collapsing, November 10, 1940, Tacoma, Washington, reproduced with permission of Corbis (© Bettmann).

We would like to thank Ryan Hines for his invaluable help in the preparation of this book.

Contents

Any words appearing in the text in bold, **like this**,
are explained in the glossary.

Lessons Learned

When buildings or structures fail, the consequences can be disastrous. If a dam wall cannot hold back the water behind it, the resulting flood can kill hundreds, perhaps thousands, of people in the valleys below. If a building or a bridge collapses, people may be sent plunging to their deaths. If a building fire is not contained and extinguished, the results can be tragic.

All of these disasters have really happened and some of them are included in this book. You can find out what went wrong and what we have learned from past mistakes. You will discover some surprising facts. For example, the Leaning Tower of Pisa continues to astound thousands of visitors every year, despite having sunk further and further into the ground for more than 800 years. Other structural failures have been spectacular, such as the Tacoma Narrows Bridge, which twisted and swayed its way to destruction.

From fail to win

After any disaster there is always an investigation into what went wrong. Many of the failures in this book have led to major changes in the way people build structures, and the way that building safety is assessed. Terrible events have often taught us valuable lessons for the future.

In this book, we have ranked the buildings, structures, and events in descending order from the quirky and interesting to some major events from which people have learned many lessons. Of course, this ranking is a matter of opinion. After reading about some of the bad ideas people have had and the mistakes they have made, you may come up with your own order of ranking.

The Boston molasses disaster

In Boston, Massachusetts, on January 15, 1919, a giant tank containing molasses suddenly exploded, sending a tide of thick goo into Boston's streets. Molasses is a brown, sticky substance that is produced when sugarcane is manufactured into sugar. In the early 1900s it was used in weapons and explosives, as well as to make alcohol for drinking.

The tank stored 8.7 million liters (2.3 million gallons) of molasses. When the tank split open, a huge wave of thick fluid moved at an estimated 56 kilometers (35 miles) per hour. The molasses crushed buildings and drowned people as it moved, killing 21 people. It turned out that leaks seen in the tank before the accident had been covered up with brown paint! The owners of the tank had to pay thousands of dollars in damages to those affected.

The destruction caused by the Boston molasses disaster was severe (see below). One positive result of the disaster was the introduction of better safety standards for construction.

The city of Pisa lies in northwest Italy. In 1063 work began on a beautiful cathedral (*duomo*) in the center of Pisa, built out of gray and white stone and lavishly decorated with marble. More than 100 years later, the Pisans decided to construct a bell tower (*campanile*) alongside their stunning cathedral. So began the story of one of the most recognizable landmarks in the world.

Tilting tower

Construction of the white marble tower began in 1173. It was designed to have 8 stories and reach 56 meters (185 feet) in height. From the very start, the engineer in charge of the project, Bonanno Pisano, had problems. The tower just would not stand straight! At first it leaned slightly to the north. Then it shifted and settled permanently to the south. By the time the first three stories were completed, the tilt to one side was already noticeable. Building work stopped after this because of a lack of construction workers. This was lucky for the tower, because it gave it time to settle. If all eight stories had been built at once, the tower would probably have toppled over!

Work on the tower did not start again until almost 100 years later. In order to try to compensate for the tower's lean, the builders made each story a little taller on the shorter side of the tower. When the bell tower was added to the top, between 1360 and 1370, it was angled slightly to the north. To this day, the slight "banana" shape of the tower is visible to the naked eye. However, nothing the builders tried worked. The tower continued to lean, although it did not fall down.

Stop the tilt!

Over the years, there have been many attempts to correct the tower's tilt and to reinforce its flimsy **foundations**. In the 1930s, under the orders of the Italian leader Benito Mussolini, tons of cement were injected into the base of the tower to try to correct its lean. However, the tower just tilted even more. By the end of the 20th century, hundreds of thousands of tourists were climbing the tower every year, and the tilt was increasing at a rate of 1.2 millimeters (0.05 inches) per year. Concerns about the tower's possible collapse led to its closure, and a committee was formed to decide how best to protect the tower for future generations.

The Leaning Tower of Pisa is the bell tower for the city's cathedral (left). Today, the tower leans at 4 meters (13 feet) from the vertical.

Soft foundations

The problems with the tower lay underground. The tower was built with foundations only 3 meters (10 feet) deep. Furthermore, it was built on a soft mixture of clay, fine sand, and shells. The weight of the tower made the structure sink into the ground unevenly. As the builders added more stories, and more weight, the tower sank further. When seven heavy, metal bells were hung in the tower in the late 1300s, their weight caused the tower to lean even further. By the time the tower was completed in the 1370s, its tilt was around 1.3 meters (51 inches) from the vertical.

This diagram shows how the tower sank over the years. As it sank, the original line and center of gravity shifted.

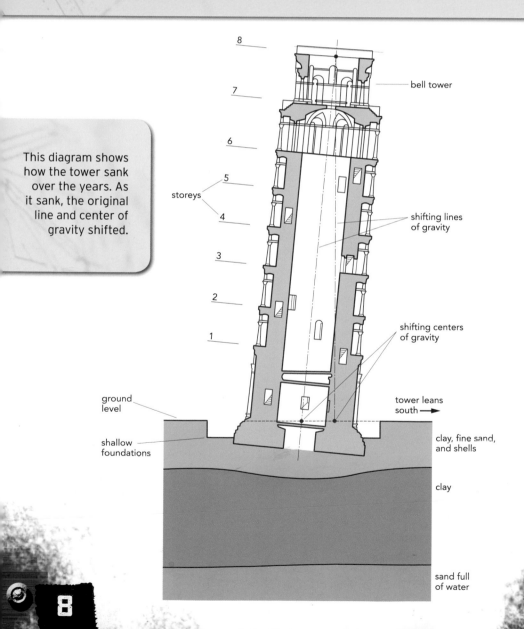

8 —
7 — bell tower
6 —
5 — storeys
4 — shifting lines of gravity
3 —
2 —
1 — shifting centers of gravity

ground level

shallow foundations

tower leans south →

clay, fine sand, and shells

clay

sand full of water

A stable future

In 1990, work began to move soil beneath the foundations from one side of the tower to the other. Very gradually the tower began to right itself, moving back 48 centimeters (19 inches) toward the vertical. Today, the engineers in charge of this project say that the tower is stable for the first time in its 800-year history. It still leans at 4 meters (13 feet) from the vertical, but it is no longer moving, and engineers expect it to stay stable for the next 200 years.

What has been learned?

The story of the Leaning Tower of Pisa shows the importance of knowing exactly what you are building on. The strongest building in the world will not survive if it is built on loose sand. Some soils change when weight is applied to them, while others have different properties depending on whether they are wet or dry. Today, before the construction of any building starts, engineers find out what is under the ground. Nobody wants to build a leaning, or worse, a collapsing skyscraper.

The most leaning structure in the world today is a church tower (pictured) in Suurhusen, Germany. The tower has tilted because its wooden foundations have rotted away.

It has been called the "worst building in the world," the "hotel of doom," and the "phantom pyramid." It is a massive building that has never been finished or used. It is by far the largest building in North Korea, and it dominates the skyline of Pyongyang, the country's capital.

Ryugyong Hotel: Vital statistics

Height:
330 meters
(1,100 feet)

Number of floors:
105

Floor space:
360,000 square meters (3.9 million square feet)

Estimated cost to date:
$750 million

Phantom pyramid

Construction of the Ryugyong Hotel began in 1987, with an estimated completion date two years later. It was intended to be the tallest hotel in the world at the time, and it was certainly much bigger than anything else ever built in the **communist** state of North Korea. Made from **reinforced concrete**, the building is shaped like a giant three-sided pyramid, with walls that slope at a 75-degree angle. At the top is a circular structure with 14 floors, some of which were intended to rotate.

The hotel was to have 3,000 rooms and should have opened in June 1989 for the World Festival of Youth and Students. It was meant to be a "prestige" project, a grand and impressive structure that would attract foreign investors to North Korea. Problems with its construction delayed the opening, and in 1992 work stopped altogether. According to the North Korean government, the funds ran out.

An embarrassment?

North Korea is a communist country under the control of its leader, Kim Jong Il. It is a very secretive country, and all forms of media, such as newspapers and television, are heavily censored. In the 1990s, the country suffered from terrible famines in which millions of people died.

Nobody knows for certain why the North Korean government decided to build such an extravagant building as the Ryugyong Hotel. The cost so far has been estimated at $750 million. Many people have questioned whether North Korea has the resources to complete such a project, and it was rumored that one reason building work stopped was because of electricity shortages. After 1992 the building was abandoned without windows or any other fittings. Many people around the world condemned it as an expensive eyesore.

It has been said of the Ryugyong Hotel that it is "hideous, dominating the Pyongyang skyline like some twisted ... version of Cinderella's castle."

FAIL!

Signs of life

In 2008 residents in Pyongyang noticed signs of life at the Ryugyong Hotel. It appears that work has started once again on the circular structure at the top. Other photographs show windows on one of the pyramid walls. An official from the North Korean government was said to have predicted that the hotel would open in 2012. Questions are still asked, however, about the wisdom of building such a huge prestige project without sufficient funds.

Beauvais Cathedral

It has been called one of the most "daring feats of **Gothic** architecture," yet it fell down twice during its construction. Today, what remains of Beauvais Cathedral in northern France continues to astound visitors with its soaring heights and exquisite architecture.

Vaults and buttresses

Beauvais Cathedral is a fine example of the Gothic style of architecture that spread across Europe in the 12th and 13th centuries. The main features of Gothic architecture are pointed arches (instead of the round arches used previously), stone roofs held up by ribbed **vaults**, and flying **buttresses**—half arches built against a wall to support them.

These diagrams show the kinds of arch, vault, and buttress that were used to create Gothic cathedrals.

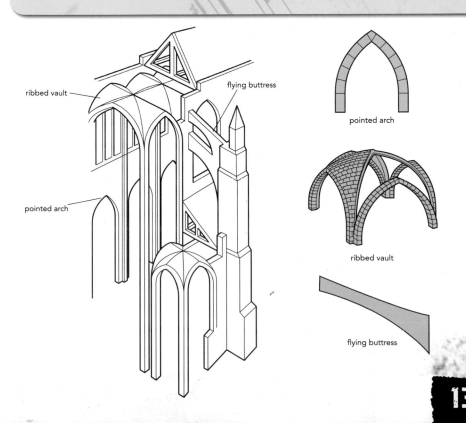

ribbed vault

flying buttress

pointed arch

pointed arch

ribbed vault

flying buttress

Ambition and failure

The ribbed vaulting of the **nave** (the main body of the church) in the cathedral of Notre Dame in Paris rises to 35 meters (115 feet). Work on this cathedral began in 1163. By the time construction began in Beauvais, in 1225, people had become even more ambitious in their desire to build higher and higher. In 1284 part of the **choir** collapsed, possibly because the spaces between the ribs were too wide. It was rebuilt with more supports over the next 50 years.

In the 16th century work began on the next stage of this massive project, the **transept** and tower. The transept is the part of a church that links the nave and choir. Once again, the builders pushed their technology to its limits, and once again the project ended in failure when the 150-meter (492-foot) tower collapsed in 1573.

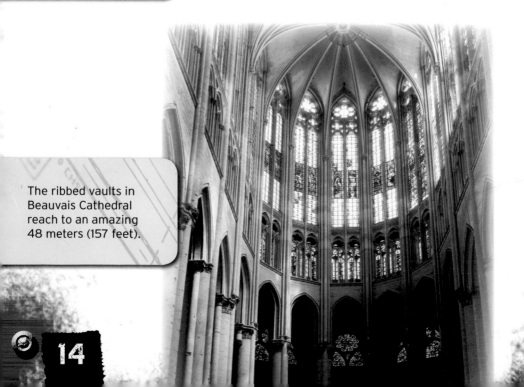

The ribbed vaults in Beauvais Cathedral reach to an amazing 48 meters (157 feet).

The congregation had just left the cathedral after a service, and there were only three people inside when the tower fell. All three escaped with their lives. This time, although the transept was repaired, the tower was abandoned. Plans to construct the massive nave were also abandoned.

What was learned?

What we can see at Beauvais Cathedral is a small part of the original plans. The desire to go higher and higher had outstripped the technology available to those 13th-, 14th-, and 15th-century builders. Modern architects and engineers have the advantage of being able to use **computer models** to test every aspect of a building long before any construction work starts. Today, the Burj Khalifa in Dubai, the world's tallest structure in 2010, rises an incredible 828 meters (2,716 feet) into the sky.

WIN!

The Burj Khalifa, seen here towering over the surrounding buildings, officially opened on January 4, 2010.

Bridges provide important links for communities all over the world. They allow people and vehicles to cross stretches of water without having to load on and off a ferry. One of the most spectacular bridges in the United States is the Sunshine Skyway in Florida. It crosses the broad mouth of Tampa Bay, linking the cities of St. Petersburg and Bradenton.

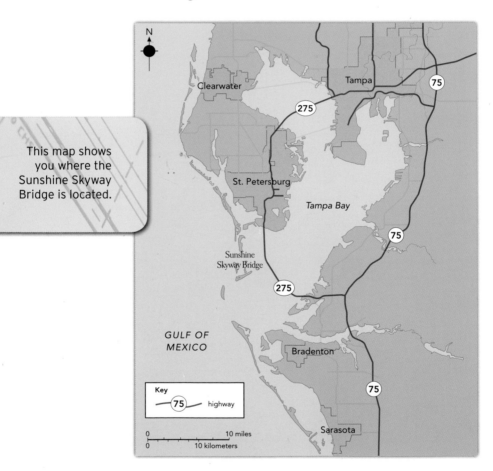

This map shows you where the Sunshine Skyway Bridge is located.

Tampa is a busy port, so many large ships must **navigate** their way past the bridge. In 1980, during a violent storm, a ship rammed into the bridge, sending more than 304 meters (1,000 feet) of road plunging into the sea. Thirty-five people died. The lessons learned from this terrible accident have since helped to make bridge structures much safer.

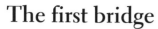

The first bridge

The first Sunshine Skyway Bridge opened in 1954. The 24-kilometer (15-mile) crossing was mainly at sea level, but part of the road was lifted up to a height of 46 meters (150 feet) above the water. This was to allow ships to pass beneath. As the amount of traffic increased, a parallel bridge was built to run alongside the old bridge. This opened in 1971. During the 1970s there were several minor accidents when ships collided with the new bridge.

The fatal morning

On May 9, 1980, a ship called *Summit Venture* was entering Tampa Bay from the Gulf of Mexico. As usual in such dangerous coastal waters, the ship was being guided by a pilot who had come on board to make sure it took the correct route along the narrow channel into the bay. The pilot's name was Captain John Lerro. He came from Tampa, and he knew the swirling waters around the Sunshine Skyway Bridge well.

Summit Venture was a **freighter**, built to carry cargo, but its holds were empty. Without any cargo, the ship rose high out of the water. As the freighter entered the bay, the weather became worse. Heavy rain made it impossible to spot important marks such as **navigation buoys**, and high winds swirled around the huge ship. As the ship made its way toward the bridge, Lerro spotted another ship—a tanker—close by on the **radar** screen.

Which is longest?

Some people believe the longest bridge in the world is in Thailand. The Bang Na Expressway is 54 kilometers (33.5 miles) long. However, it is not crossing water for much of its length.

This makes many people rank the Lake Pontchartrain Causeway in Louisiana as the longest bridge. The causeway is made up of two bridges, the longest of which is 38.4 kilometers (23.9 miles) long.

Disaster strikes

Lerro had to make some difficult decisions very quickly. He could not anchor and ride out the storm because of the tanker moving toward him. He could not stop his engines and wait for better visibility because the wind was too strong and the ship would have been out of control. He decided to approach the bridge, but he did not realize that the very strong wind had pushed him off course. He needed to steer a course marked by two navigation buoys that would take him safely through the center of the bridge.

When the ship was blown off course, however, it headed toward the part of the bridge that held up the road above. At 7:38 a.m., as the storm cleared for a moment, Lerro saw the bridge looming up in front of the ship. He ordered the engines to be put into reverse and the anchors to be thrown out, but it was too late. A minute later the freighter crashed into the bridge.

When the *Summit Venture* struck the Sunshine Skyway Bridge, a car skidded to a halt only inches away from the broken edge.

The impact of the collision brought down a section of the road together with the vehicles traveling along it. They included a Greyhound bus carrying 26 people, and several cars. One car landed on the bow of the *Summit Venture* then rolled into the sea. Amazingly, its driver survived, but 35 other people lost their lives as a result of the collision.

What was learned?

The construction of a new bridge began soon after the accident. Improved safety was the major concern. Most bridges were unprotected against ship collisions. The solution was to build large concrete islands, called dolphins, around the piers that support the bridge. This means that any ship going off course near the bridge would collide with a dolphin rather than the actual bridge. The bridge designers also installed monitoring systems so that the traffic can be stopped quickly if there is a problem on the bridge. The safety lessons learned from the Sunshine Skyway Bridge accident were also applied to other bridges across the United States.

WIN!

The new Sunshine Skyway Bridge opened in 1987. It is bigger, better, and a lot safer than the old bridge.

Ronan Point Tower Collapse

On the morning of May 16, 1968, Ivy Hodge woke up and went to her kitchen as usual to make a cup of tea. She lived in an apartment on the 18th floor of a new high-rise called Ronan Point in east London, England.

Hodge struck a match to light the gas flame of her stove, and instantly an explosion knocked her unconscious. The explosion also blew out the walls of her apartment and caused the collapse of the entire corner of the building.

Lucky escape

One resident of Ronan Point had an unbelievably lucky escape. She was lying on the couch when the outer wall collapsed. She struggled to the door as the floor disappeared beneath her feet, leaving her stranded on a narrow ledge. The door was blocked with rubble, but her husband managed to grab her through a small gap. While holding onto her with one arm, he desperately cleared rubble with the other. He rescued her, injured but alive.

Falling dominoes

Amazingly, Hodge survived the explosion and the collapse. When she regained consciousness, she was lying in a pool of water on the floor of her kitchen with devastation all around. The explosion destroyed the outer walls of the apartment, which were the only support for the walls above. This caused the four floors above, including the top floor, to collapse.

As these floors fell, their weight landed on the floors below, causing floor 17 to smash into floor 16, and so on, all the way to the ground floor, like a set of falling dominoes. Four people were killed and seventeen were injured. Hodge suffered burns from the explosion.

Layout of Apartment 90

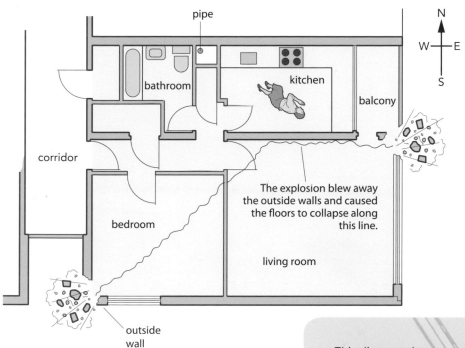

The explosion blew away the outside walls and caused the floors to collapse along this line.

This diagram shows you the layout of Apartment 90, on the 18th floor of Ronan Point, where Ivy Hodge lived.

Housing shortage

The story leading up to this terrible disaster starts just after World War II (1939–1945). Bombs dropped from aircraft had destroyed large areas of many cities, and there was a terrible shortage of housing in many places. London had suffered extensive bombing during attacks by the German air force during the **Blitz**. Huge areas of the city lay in ruins.

The need for housing that could be built quickly and cheaply led to the popularity of high-rise apartment complexes. Apartments were built on top of each other to create buildings many stories high, such as Ronan Point. People were often glad to move from old, overcrowded houses to the brand-new, modern convenience of an apartment in the sky.

The Larsen-Nielsen system

Ronan Point had been completed only three months before the disaster, and it was the second of nine identical high-rises that were due to be built. The tower was constructed using a technique developed in Denmark called the Larsen-Nielsen system. This system allowed buildings to be erected quickly and cheaply. Room-sized concrete panels were made in a factory, then bolted together and stacked up on top of each other to make towers of apartments.

FAIL!

Each concrete wall of Ronan Point supported the wall above it. If one wall was suddenly removed, the wall above had no support. This is what resulted in the **progressive collapse** of the corner of the building.

What was learned?

The corner of Ronan Point that had collapsed was rebuilt, and the whole building was reinforced. Gas was also banned from the tower to remove the risk of explosions. Electricity was used instead. The story did not end there. Architects and residents continued to voice their concerns about the building, especially about the dangers from high winds and fire. Eventually the building was found to have major cracks, probably caused by the stresses of high winds. In 1986 Ronan Point was demolished. Unusually, it was not blown up, but rather dismantled floor by floor so that it could be studied.

It was found that the tower had been built in an unsatisfactory way, with nuts not screwed down, spaces filled with garbage instead of mortar, and not enough reinforced steel used to support the wall panels. As a result of these findings, many other high-rise buildings built in the same way in the United Kingdom were also demolished in the years that followed. People also learned lessons about the need for quality control while a building is being constructed. Even the best designs are worse than useless if the quality of the actual workmanship on the building is poor. Skilled and qualified inspectors are needed to oversee buildings as they are being constructed.

Redundancy

The collapse of Ronan Point led to building regulations being reviewed and tightened all over the world. The gas leak that initially caused the explosion was the result of installation errors. Despite the fact that the explosion was not terribly powerful, it had managed to blow out the entire wall of Ivy Hodge's apartment. Worse, once that wall was removed there was nothing to prevent the collapse of the wall above. Architects and engineers call this **"redundancy."** This is the principle that if one safety measure fails, there should be another to take its place.

At 7:05 a.m. on November 21, 1980, an employee of the MGM Grand Hotel in Las Vegas, Nevada, let himself into the Deli, one of the five restaurants near the hotel's **casino**. The restaurant was not yet open, as most of the hotel's 3,400 guests were still in their rooms in the high-rise towers above the casino. The employee saw that a sheet of flame was reaching up one wall from floor to ceiling. He ran for help and for a fire extinguisher. By the time he returned, the heat was so intense that he was unable to enter the Deli.

Las Vegas

Las Vegas began as an **oasis** in the Mojave Desert. *Las Vegas* means "the meadows" in Spanish. Settlers moved there in the 19th century, and the city was founded in 1905. It has become famous around the world for its casinos.

Fireball

As the fire spread, other hotel employees tried to extinguish the flames. The first fire engine arrived at 7:17 a.m. The firefighters were met by thick, black smoke pouring out of the Deli. As they approached the restaurant a massive fireball burst out and rolled into the hotel's casino.

This diagram shows you how the MGM Grand Hotel fire spread throughout the building.

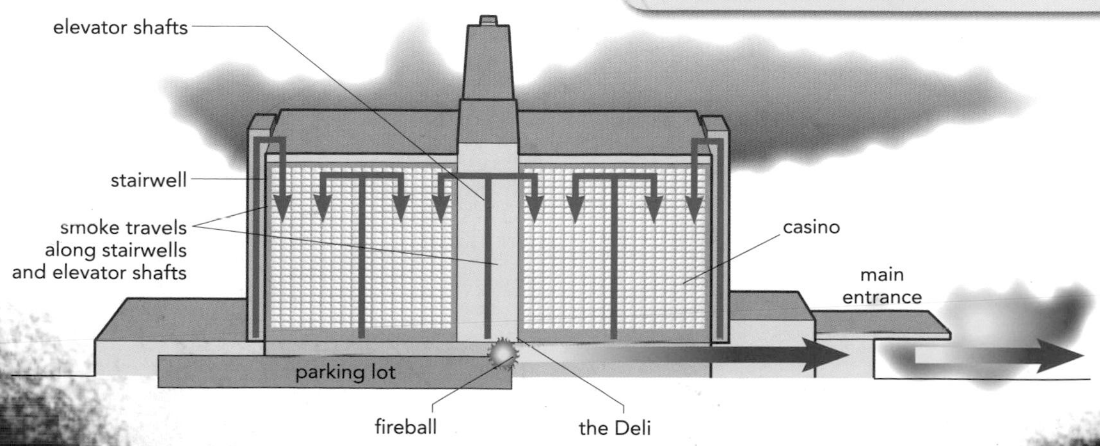

elevator shafts

stairwell

smoke travels along stairwells and elevator shafts

casino

main entrance

parking lot

fireball

the Deli

It was later found that the fire raced through the casino at a
speed of 4.5–6 meters (15–19 feet) per second, fueled by wall
coverings, furniture, and plastic fixtures. Seven people died inside
the casino itself. The fire blew out the doors of the hotel's main
entrance and engulfed the hotel lobby.

Flames

Neither the casino nor the hotel's restaurants were equipped with
sprinkler systems. These systems spray water if they sense heat,
and they are designed to prevent the spread of fire. The hotel
building itself did have a sprinkler system, and this helped
firefighters to contain the spread of the flames, and to prevent
the fire from engulfing the hotel.

Smoke

What the firefighters and sprinkler systems could not do was stop the spread of the thick, black smoke pouring from the casino. As the plastic fixtures and fittings in the casino burned, they produced a **toxic** smoke that quickly spread through the hotel building. The smoke raced up stairwells and elevator shafts, and was pumped through the hotel's ventilation system.

Rescue workers tried to get as many guests and employees out of the burning building as possible.

Panic

Most of the hotel's guests were unaware of the fire until smoke began to enter their rooms. There was no automatic fire alarm, and the manual system had been destroyed by the flames. Panicking guests ran to the stairwells to try to escape downward, only to find that the doors locked behind them and that they became trapped. Other guests broke the glass in the hotel windows or moved onto their balconies to try to escape the choking smoke. At least one person died trying to jump to safety.

Sprinkler systems

In total, 85 people died in the MGM Grand Hotel fire, most from smoke inhalation (breathing in smoke). Some died in their sleep, unaware of the danger that had engulfed them. In the investigation that was held after the fire, it became clear that the disaster could easily have been prevented. When the hotel was built in 1972, fire marshals had tried to insist on the installation of sprinkler systems in the restaurant and casino areas. The hotel was unwilling to pay the estimated $192,000 bill for these extra systems. It was argued that the casino and restaurants were open 24 hours a day, so in the event of a fire there would always be someone present to raise the alarm and deal with it.

What was learned?

If there had been a sprinkler system in the Deli, it is likely that the fire would have been extinguished immediately. It was also found that a defect in the hotel's ventilation system meant that it continued pumping toxic smoke around the building long after it should have shut down. Nobody was ever given a **criminal conviction** for the fire, but around $223 million in damages was paid to those affected. Lessons were also learned about the dangers of smoke. Most of those who died were far from any flames, but were instead killed by breathing in toxic fumes. The MGM Grand Hotel was rebuilt with sprinkler systems throughout and an automatic fire alarm. Today, it is called Bally's Las Vegas.

Another fire

Only 81 days after the Grand Hotel disaster, an **arsonist** set fire to the Las Vegas Hilton Hotel. This time firefighters made use of the knowledge they had gained from the MGM disaster. Local television news bulletins were used to advise people to stay in their rooms until they were rescued. As a result of both of these fires, there was a major review of fire safety in all high-rise buildings.

Too Much Snow

Public buildings such as sports stadiums, theaters, or convention centers are often designed with wide, single-span roofs to create a large, uninterrupted space inside. These buildings are often very dramatic to look at. It is important for such structures to be tested for all weather conditions. If they are not, the results can be disastrous, as was discovered in January 2006.

FAIL!

The roof of the ice rink in Bad Reichenhall, Germany, collapsed from the weight of snow on it.

Weight of snow

During the winter of 2005–2006, many countries in Europe experienced higher amounts of snowfall than usual. As layers of snow and ice build up on the roof of a building, they put extra pressure on the roof structure. Building regulations allow for this extra weight, so that roofs are constructed to be strong enough to carry the load. Countries such as Germany also have strict rules about how much snow can build up on a roof before it has to be cleared.

On Monday, January 2, 2006, heavy snow fell on the town of Bad Reichenhall in southern Germany. The area is popular for winter sports, so the snow was not unusual. As the snow accumulated on the roof of the town's ice rink, a decision was made to close the building. Yet when the roof suddenly caved in at around 4:00 p.m., there were still people in the building. Fifty people were trapped in the rubble in freezing temperatures. Fifteen people died.

What was learned?

Investigations after the disaster found that the roof should have been able to support the weight of the snow on it—around 20 centimeters (8 inches). The problem lay in design flaws and the lack of any inspection system to make sure the building was safe.

The ice rink was opened in 1971, and its roof was supported by timber **girders**. The initial designs had not been properly checked. Investigators also showed that the extremes of temperature and humidity in the ice rink had gradually affected the timber girders, but as there were no regular inspections, nobody had noticed this. Two years later the engineer, architect, and head of construction all stood trial for the disaster.

The Millennium Dome

The O2 Arena (left) in London, originally called the Millennium Dome, has a huge plastic roof held up by steel cables attached to 12 masts. The roof is designed to minimize the dangers from rainwater or snow collecting on it. It also has **redundancy** built in, so that if one cable were to fall, others would be able to carry the extra load.

Katowice, 2006

Later in the same month, another major roof collapse happened, this time in the city of Katowice, in Poland. Once again, heavy snowfall was the problem. The roof collapse was at the Katowice International Fair, an exhibition center designed to hold hundreds of people. The roof caved in at around 5:15 p.m., during an international racing pigeon exhibition.

There were around 500 people in this hall at the time of the collapse in Katowice. In total, 66 people died.

FAIL!

Just as at Bad Reichenhall, it seemed that bad design and lack of inspection were major problems. Even worse, the roof of the building had shown signs of being unable to withstand the weight of snow before the accident, yet the organizers had gone ahead regardless. As a result of the disaster, the architects, a building inspector, and several people in charge of the building were put on trial in 2009.

After the lessons learned from these roof collapses, building regulations in both Germany and Poland were tightened. In particular, the importance of continuing safety checks on public buildings was recognized.

The Kemper Arena

The Kemper Arena in Kansas City, Missouri, had a large, flat concrete roof, 97 meters (318 feet) wide by 108 meters (354 feet) long. The roof was held up by an exterior frame. It was designed to hold water during a rainstorm and to release it into the city's **storm sewers**.

Despite this, on June 4, 1979, a violent rainstorm and high winds overloaded the roof. Unable to take the strain, the supports holding up the roof broke and a large section of it collapsed. Luckily there was nobody in the arena at the time. Afterward the design flaws in the roof were quickly identified and corrected, and the arena opened once again in 1981.

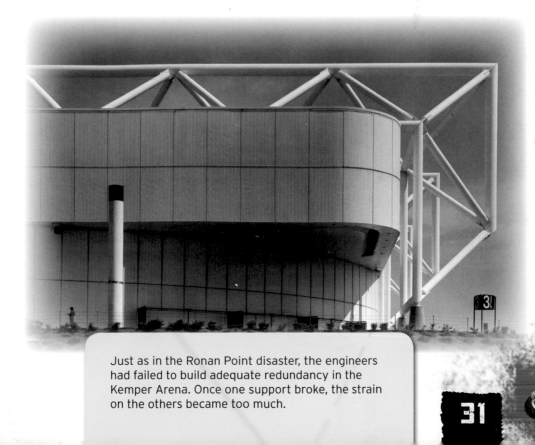

Just as in the Ronan Point disaster, the engineers had failed to build adequate redundancy in the Kemper Arena. Once one support broke, the strain on the others became too much.

The Hyatt Regency Hotel

In July 1980 the Hyatt Regency Hotel in Kansas City, Missouri, opened for business. It was one of the most luxurious and spectacular hotels to be built in the United States at the time. The hotel had three separate buildings that were connected by a large covered space, called an **atrium**. The atrium was crisscrossed by three walkways that allowed people to move from one building to another at the level of the second, third, and fourth floors. The fourth-floor walkway was directly above the one on the second floor.

Walkway collapse

On July 17, 1981, the hotel was full of people enjoying a dance contest. The atrium itself held about 1,600 people, many of them dancing to the band on the ground floor. Others crowded onto the walkways to get a better view of the scene below. Suddenly there was a loud crack. One of the supports holding the fourth-floor walkway had given way. Within seconds the other supports had also failed. The walkway fell, taking the second-floor walkway with it. Together both walkways and the people on them smashed into the crowd below. Altogether 114 people were killed, and more than 200 were badly injured. It was the worst structural building failure ever experienced in the United States.

In this picture, you can see the wreckage of two collapsed walkways in the Hyatt Regency Hotel.

Design flaw

Only days later, investigators had already uncovered the design flaw that was mainly responsible for the disaster. In the original designs, both walkways were to be attached to long rods hung from the frame of the atrium roof. These rods were to be continuous from the second-floor walkway to the roof. The steel company supplying the rods changed the design. Shorter rods were used, one connecting from the fourth-floor walkway to the roof, and a separate rod connecting the second-floor walkway to the fourth. This meant that the beam of the fourth-floor walkway was supporting its own weight and the weight of the second-floor walkway.

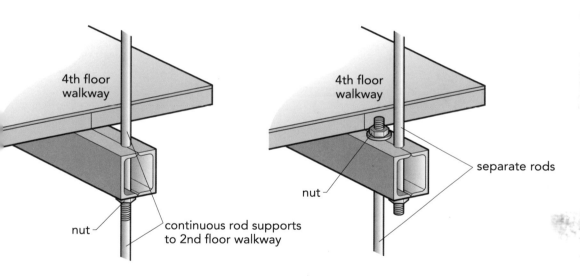

Original design
Connection supports weight of walkway

Final design
Connection supports weight of walkway plus walkway below

This diagram shows the difference between the original design of the walkways in the Hyatt Regency Hotel and the flawed, final design.

What was learned?

After the disaster, the steel company said that it had informed the engineers in charge of construction about the change to the design of the rods. The engineers denied any knowledge of the change, despite the fact that the new designs were stamped with their approval. It was later found that even the first design with the continuous rod would not have satisfied the Kansas City building code that sets standards and safety levels for construction.

A lawyer named Patrick McLarney represented the state of Missouri against the builders of the Hyatt Regency Hotel. He said:

"Nobody ever did any calculations to figure out whether or not the particular connection that held the skywalks up would work. It got built without anybody ever figuring out if it would be strong enough. It just slipped through the cracks…"

As a result of the findings about the Hyatt Regency disaster, the engineering company responsible for the construction of the hotel lost its license to practice. The case brought up lots of questions about who was ultimately responsible for checking the safety of building designs and approving them. It also highlighted the need to ensure that what was planned on paper translated into what was actually built. The end result was changes to building codes to make sure that everyone—architects, engineers, suppliers, and builders—knows their responsibilities, in order to avoid a repeat of such a tragedy.

Lessons not learned

The Sampoong Superstore in Seoul, South Korea, opened in December 1989. It became very popular, and its owners decided to add a fifth floor to the four-story building.

On June 29, 1995, cracks on the fifth floor became so bad that the store had to be shut to the public. Several experts inspected the building and declared it unsafe. Despite this, the managers did not close the store, because they did not want to lose any money. Even when the ceilings on the fourth floor began to sink, trade did not stop. Only when the whole structure began to crack did the evacuation begin.

It was too late. When the building collapsed, hundreds of shoppers and employees were still inside. Around 500 people died. The disaster provoked outrage and led to a major review of safety standards in South Korea.

Atrium facts

The world's largest atrium is in the pyramid-shaped Luxor Hotel in Las Vegas. The hotel rooms line the inside of the sloping pyramid walls.

The world's tallest atrium is in Burj Al Arab in Dubai. This luxury hotel is shaped like a sail and stands on an artificial island. Inside, its atrium rises 180 meters (590 feet).

The Tacoma Narrows Bridge opened in 1940. It was nicknamed the "bouncing bridge" and "Galloping Gertie" because of its swaying and rolling movements. People came from far and wide to experience the unsettling roller coaster ride as they crossed from one side to the other. Many reported seeing cars ahead of them on the bridge disappear and reappear, as if riding a large wave. It stood for just four months before collapsing during a windstorm.

Bridging Puget Sound

The Tacoma Narrows Bridge was built to link the town of Tacoma with Gig Harbor on the Olympic Peninsula in Washington state. The bridge spanned the treacherous waters of the Puget Sound, which at that point is about 1.5 kilometers (1 mile) wide. For many years, a ferry service connected the two communities.

However, in the 1920s and 1930s, cars became increasingly popular, so people wanted to be able to drive from one place to the other. The route by road from Tacoma to Gig Harbor was 170 kilometers (107 miles). Once the bridge was built, this distance would be just 13 kilometers (8 miles).

The problem was, who would pay for such an expensive project? Private companies did not believe there would be enough traffic to make the bridge pay for itself. In the end, it was the threat of war that led to the construction of the bridge.

"I saw the Narrows Bridge die today, and only by the grace of God, escaped dying with it…

"I decided the bridge was breaking up and my only hope was to get back to shore. On hands and knees most of the time, I crawled 500 yards or more to the towers…"

–Leonard Coatsworth, news editor of the *Tacoma News Tribune*

In response to developments in Nazi Germany and elsewhere, the U.S. government began to pour millions of dollars into defense. One of the biggest U.S. Navy shipyards was in Bremerton, on the Olympic Peninsula, while the U.S. Air Force established important airfields near Tacoma. Suddenly, a bridge to link the mainland and the peninsula seemed far more important.

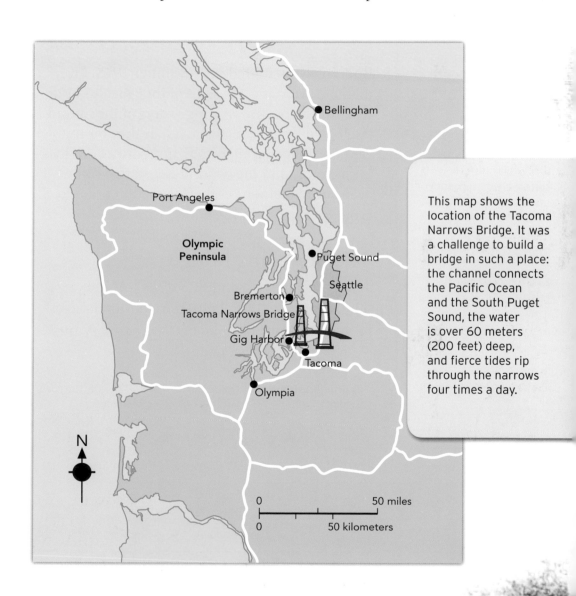

This map shows the location of the Tacoma Narrows Bridge. It was a challenge to build a bridge in such a place: the channel connects the Pacific Ocean and the South Puget Sound, the water is over 60 meters (200 feet) deep, and fierce tides rip through the narrows four times a day.

Long and narrow

A design for a bridge was drawn up by a local engineer, and it was estimated that it would cost $11 million. However, the Washington State Toll Bridge Authority decided that a different engineer, Leon Moisseiff, should design the bridge. His **suspension bridge** was much lighter, narrower, and cheaper.

Building work started in November 1938. Over the next two years, the sight of the graceful bridge reaching across the swirling waters of the Sound fascinated local residents. Even as they built it, workers noticed a characteristic "bounce" as the bridge moved in the wind. It is said that some even sucked lemons as they worked in order to avoid getting motion sickness!

The bouncing bridge

The bridge opened on July 1, 1940. At the time, it was the third-longest suspension bridge in the world (see table below).

Moisseiff's bridge

The main span of Moisseiff's bridge (between the two supporting towers) was 850 meters (2,800 feet) long. That was 72 times longer than its width, which was much more than any bridge ever built. Moisseiff was following a trend that allowed suspension bridges to be built using less steel, which made them cheaper. Even before work on the bridge started, some people thought Moisseiff's design was fundamentally unsound.

	George Washington Bridge	Golden Gate Bridge	Tacoma Narrows Bridge
Year completed	1935	1937	1940
Cost (U.S. dollars)	59.5 million	35 million	6.4 million
Length (meters/feet)	1,060/3,478	1,273/4,177	850/2,789
Depth (meters/feet)	11.0/36.1	7.6/24.9	2.4/7.9
Width (meters/feet)	32/105	27/89	12/39

People had to pay a toll to use the bridge. Despite this, it was a huge success. In the four months that the bridge stood, more than 260,000 vehicles crossed from one side to the other. Many people came simply for a thrill—because even in light winds, the bridge moved.

The Toll Bridge Authority was concerned about its bouncing bridge. It appointed Professor F. Bert Farquharson to try to come up with a solution. He made a scale model of the bridge and studied it carefully. Several changes were made in an attempt to lessen the bridge's movements, including cables that were attached from the side spans to secure anchorages.

This photograph shows the bridge twisting. Many people paid the toll to cross the bridge just for the excitement of the ride.

The sad tale of Tubby

Professor Farquharson was a dog-lover. At around 10:55 a.m. he stumbled to Coatsworth's car in the middle of the bridge. He tried to take hold of the dog inside, named Tubby, but the terrified animal bit his finger. Farquharson had to leave Tubby behind. He reached safety with only seconds to spare. Suddenly, half of the center span of the bridge broke free from its cables and plunged with a thunderous roar into the waves below. Coatsworth's car, with Tubby inside, went with it.

On November 7, 1940, strong winds started the now familiar "galloping" movement of the bridge. Just before 10 a.m. Leonard Coatsworth, a news editor at the *Tacoma News Tribune*, drove on to the bridge. In the back of his car was his daughter's dog. Suddenly the road made a violent movement that sent the car sliding uncontrollably. Coatsworth scrambled out and began to crawl along the bucking, rolling road. The road was now not only rippling up and down but also twisting from side to side.

Professor Farquharson walked out to the East Tower of the bridge and started to take pictures of the swaying bridge. Coatsworth, meanwhile, had reached the tollbooth at the end of the bridge and told the attendant about the dog trapped in his car (see box at left).

Farquharson believed that the bridge would weather the storm. He said later, "Though the bridge was bucking up at an angle of 45 degrees, I thought she would be able to fight it out. But, that wasn't to be."

FAIL!

The Tacoma Narrows Bridge collapsed violently into Puget Sound.

Too flexible

Leon Moisseiff declared that he was "completely at a loss to explain the collapse" of the Tacoma Narrows Bridge. The failure effectively ended his career, and he died only three years later. Meanwhile, it became apparent that his bridge design, although graceful, had completely ignored the effects the wind would have on such a lightweight and narrow structure. The bridge was just too flexible. Once it began to twist sideways, the twist would lead to more twisting. Eventually the forces on the cables holding the roadway in place became too much.

The replacement bridge was opened in the same place in 1950. Eventually, there was so much traffic that a second, parallel bridge (left) opened in 2007.

The lessons learned

The collapse of the bridge was a disaster, but it taught bridge-builders many valuable lessons. It took another 10 years before the second Tacoma Narrows Bridge opened, years that were spent thoroughly researching the design of suspension bridges. Wind tunnels were already widely used to test aircraft. Now a special wind tunnel was built at the University of Washington to test the effects of wind on bridges. It was the first time that a wind tunnel had been used in this way. Before any building work started on the second bridge, a scale model was constructed and tested in the wind tunnel. The tests took four years, as the model was changed and improved. The new bridge opened to traffic on October 14, 1950. The research that went into its construction changed the way suspension bridges were designed and built forever.

Another wobbly bridge

The London Millennium Footbridge is a steel suspension footbridge across the Thames River. It opened in June 2000. The bridge swayed sideways up to 7 centimeters (3 inches). This wobble came from the footsteps of people crossing. The wobble was uncomfortable, so people tried to walk in time with it—but this only increased the sway. After more research, engineers fitted "dampers" to absorb the movement.

The London Millennium Footbridge reopened in 2002 and has not wobbled since.

The St. Francis Dam

The city of Los Angeles, California, was founded in 1781, and it grew rapidly during the second half of the 19th century. In 1850 it had a population of 1,600, and by 1900 the number of people living in the city was around 100,000. However, by this time it was clear to many that the city could not expand any further without increasing its supplies of an essential resource—water.

The mighty aqueduct

The people of Los Angeles relied on water taken from the Los Angeles River as well as occasional rainfall. In 1908 construction began on a massive **aqueduct**, which was designed to carry water in pipes from the Owens Valley, over 320 kilometers (200 miles) north of the city. The chief engineer in charge of the project was William Mulholland. He was an immigrant from Ireland who had started his working life as a ditch cleaner for the Los Angeles City Water Company. He had worked his way up the ranks until he became head of the newly established Los Angeles Department of Water in 1902.

William Mulholland helped Los Angeles grow into one of the largest cities in the United States.

Success or disaster?

Mulholland's aqueduct was completed in 1913, and it was a huge success for the people of Los Angeles. It was, however, disastrous for the farmers and ranchers in the Owens Valley. Much of the water from the Owens Lake and river was now diverted along the aqueduct to the city, and by 1924 Owens Lake had completely dried up. In that year a group of ranchers took matters into their own hands and blew up a section of the aqueduct, sparking the "Owens Valley War." The **sabotage** continued until 1927, when financial ruin finally brought an end to farming in the Owens Valley.

This map shows you where the St. Francis Dam was located, and where the Los Angeles aqueduct still is.

Meanwhile, Mulholland was busy on another project, this time to protect the city's water supply from problems such as sabotage, drought, or earthquake. The aqueduct ran through the San Francisquito Canyon, about 48 kilometers (30 miles) north of Los Angeles. Mulholland thought that this canyon was the ideal site for a dam and a reservoir to store water for the city. In 1924 work started on the St. Francis Dam.

Dam design

Mulholland originally designed the dam to stand 53 meters (175 feet) high, but just after construction began he decided to add another 3 meters (10 feet) to the top of the dam wall. This would increase the amount of water that could be trapped behind the dam. Then in 1925, with the population of Los Angeles still rising and the demand for water growing ever greater, Mulholland added another 3 meters (10 feet) to the dam, taking the dam wall to 59 meters (195 feet) in height. It was now necessary to build two huge extra walls, or dikes, on either side of the main dam to contain all the extra water held back in the reservoir.

Look closely at this photograph. You can see how large the St. Francis Dam was compared to the people in the picture.

Worrying leaks

The reservoir began to fill in 1926, but it did not reach its full capacity until March 1928. On March 12, Tony Harnischfeger, the dam keeper who was in charge of the upkeep of the dam, asked Mulholland to inspect various leaks through the dam wall. It was a windy day, and the reservoir was so full that water was being blown over the top of the wall. Mulholland inspected the leaks and gave his opinion that the dam was safe. He knew that some degree of leakage from a dam was normal.

A wall of water

Just before midnight on March 12, 1928, a man named Ace Hopewell passed the dam on his way to work further upstream. About half a mile beyond the dam, he suddenly felt a tremendous rumbling and heard the sound of crashing in the distance. He assumed it was an earthquake. In fact, he was the last survivor to see the St. Francis Dam intact.

This section of the dam wall was all that remained after the structure collapsed. It became known as the "tombstone."

The dam collapsed, sending a wall of water down into the valley below. Tony Harnischfeger and his family were probably the first to die as the water overwhelmed their home in the valley just below the dam. The wave rose over 30 meters (100 feet) high, and as the water gathered pace it destroyed everything in its path. The deadly flood of water, mud, and debris traveled 87 kilometers (54 miles) until it reached the Pacific Ocean. It is not known exactly how many people were killed, but the official death toll was 495. Many bodies were recovered from the ocean.

Investigations into the disaster

In the weeks after the disaster, there were several state investigations to find out why the dam collapsed. These and later studies have shown that there were several possible factors that contributed to the disaster. Unknown to Mulholland, the dam had been built across a fault line in the ground. This was a place where an earthquake was likely to occur. However, it was not an earthquake that toppled the dam.

Scientists found that one side of the dam was built on rock and soil that formed part of a huge, ancient landslide. When this rock and soil became wet, it also became unstable. It was the movement of this earth that cracked the dam wall. Mulholland's decision to raise the height of the dam without sufficiently altering the design of the wall also contributed to its failure.

Eyewitness

A local man named Ray Rising managed to survive, but his wife and three daughters were all killed in the catastrophic flood. This is his description of his escape:

"I heard a roaring like a cyclone … The water was so high we couldn't get out the front door … In the darkness I became tangled in an oak tree, fought clear and swam to the surface … I grabbed the roof of another house, jumping off when it floated to the hillside…"

Malpasset disaster

Construction on the Malpasset Dam in southern France began in 1941. It was a thin, concrete dam built in an arch shape to hold back the water of the Reyran River. The **foundations** of the dam failed suddenly and catastrophically on December 2, 1959. The entire dam collapsed, sending a massive wave that destroyed two villages and flooded part of the town of Fréjus, about 10 kilometers (6 miles) away. It is thought that 433 people died in this disaster.

End of a career

Mulholland was a broken man after the St. Francis Dam disaster. He took all the blame upon himself and retired from his job. He died in 1935. At the **inquest** into the dam failure he said: "Don't blame anyone else. Whatever fault there was on the job, put it on me…"

What was learned?

A major lesson was learned from this disaster: never again should the design and construction of such a project be left to one person. People also began to realize the importance of finding out about the **geology** of the site of a proposed dam. Nobody at the time knew that the dam had been constructed across a fault in the land, nor that the ancient landslide holding the dam wall would crumble once it was immersed in water.

Another dam built in California by Mulholland, called the Mulholland Dam, was reinforced directly after the disaster in case it also failed. Other dam projects were reassessed and redesigned in the light of the disaster, and the first dam safety agency was established. The failure of the St. Francis Dam was a terrible tragedy for the hundreds of people who lost their lives, but in the long term it made dam-building safer.

Vaiont landslide

In 1963 the Vaiont Dam, in Italy, was the second-highest dam in the world, standing 262 meters (858 feet) tall. The reservoir behind the dam was still being filled with water when the entire slope on one side of the reservoir collapsed.

The impact of the landslide sent a wave of water over the top of the dam and down the valley below, destroying the village of Longarone and killing nearly 2,000 people. It later emerged that warnings about the unstable slopes and soil movements had been ignored by the dam-builders. The dam still stands, but it is no longer used to store water.

This photograph shows the devastation left in Longarone after the collapse of the Vaiont Dam.

Timeline

1163   Construction of Notre Dame Cathedral begins in
       Paris, France

1173   Construction begins on the cathedral bell tower in
       Pisa, Italy

1225   Construction of Beauvais Cathedral begins in France

1370s Completion of the Leaning Tower of Pisa

1573   Tower of Beauvais Cathedral collapses

1913   Opening of the Los Angeles **aqueduct**, in California

1919   Boston molasses disaster, in Boston, Massachusetts

1928   Failure of St. Francis Dam, in California, kills
       495 people

1940   Opening of Tacoma Narrows Bridge, in Washington
       state. The bridge collapses four months later.

1954   Opening of first Sunshine Skyway Bridge, in Florida

1959   Failure of Malpasset Dam, in France, kills more than
       400 people

1963   Landslide into the reservoir of the Vaiont Dam, in Italy,
       kills around 2,000 people

1968   Collapse of Ronan Point apartment tower in London,
       England, kills four people

1973   Opening of new headquarters of Standard Oil company,
       in Chicago, Illinois

1979   Roof collapse at Kemper Arena, in Kansas City, Missouri

1980   Sunshine Skyway Bridge accident kills 35 people

1980   Fire at MGM Grand Hotel, in Las Vegas, Nevada, kills
        85 people

1981   Walkway collapse at Hyatt Regency Hotel in Kansas City,
        Missouri, kills 114 people

1981   Fire at Las Vegas Hilton Hotel kills eight people

1986   Ronan Point high rise is demolished

1987   Construction of Ryugyong Hotel begins in Pyongyang,
        North Korea

1987   Opening of the new Sunshine Skyway Bridge

1990   Work begins to stabilize the Leaning Tower of Pisa

1990   Work begins to replace 43,000 sheets of **cladding** on
        the Amoco headquarters

1992   Construction of Ryugyong Hotel stops

1995   Sampoong Superstore, in Seoul, South Korea, collapses,
        killing around 500 people

2006   Heavy snowfall leads to roof collapses in Katowice,
        Poland, and Bad Reichenhall, Germany

2008   Work restarts on Ryugyong Hotel

2010   Official opening of Burj Khalifa, which stands at
        828 meters (2,716 feet) high

Glossary

aqueduct bridge used to carry water

arsonist someone who deliberately starts a fire

atrium large, open space in a building. Atriums are often several stories high.

Blitz bombing of London and other cities in the United Kingdom by the German air force in 1940–1941

buttress support built against a wall to hold it up

casino public room or building for gambling

choir part of the church nearest the main altar

cladding covering of a structure

communist political system, or a person who supports such a system, in which all property is owned by the community

computer model model of a system or a structure on a computer that is used to test how the system or structure would behave in real life

criminal conviction judgment at the end of a trial that finds someone guilty of a crime

foundation lowest part of a building, usually below ground, that bears the weight of the building

freighter large ship designed to carry cargo

geology science of the structure of Earth

girder large beam

Gothic describes a style of architecture that spread across Europe in the 12th and 13th centuries

hydroelectric power electricity produced using the energy from fast-flowing or falling water

inquest investigation after an incident or accident to find out what happened

nave central part of a church

navigate plan and find a route, most usually used for ships and aircraft

navigation buoy colored float that is used to mark a channel or other feature in coastal waters

oasis green and fertile place in the middle of the desert

progressive collapse in engineering, this term describes a situation in which the failure of one part leads to the collapse of others, resulting in a structural failure far greater than the original cause

radar **Ra**dio **De**tection **a**nd **R**anging, an electronic system for detecting ships and aircraft by bouncing radio waves off them and receiving the reflections. Radar also shows the direction and speed of ships and aircraft.

redundancy in engineering, the principle that if one safety measure fails, there should be another to take its place

reinforced concrete concrete that has metal rods embedded in it to strengthen it

sabotage act of deliberately destroying or damaging something

storm sewer drain designed to carry excess water at times of heavy rainfall

suspension bridge bridge in which the deck or road is held up with cables suspended from towers

toxic highly poisonous

transept crossways part of a church that links the nave and choir

vault roof in the form of an arch, or a series of arches

Find Out More

Books

Bos, Samone, and Phil Wilkinson. *Super Structures*. New York: Dorling Kindersley, 2008.

Oxlade, Chris. *Building Amazing Structures* series, 2nd edn. Chicago: Heinemann Library, 2006.

Structural Wonders series. New York: Weigl, 2009–2010.

Websites

www.pbs.org/wgbh/nova/bridge/build.html
This website lets you pretend to be a bridge engineer. Play a game in which you decide what kind of construction is right for your site. Click on "Suspension bridge" to learn more about the Tacoma Narrows Bridge and to see videos of it swaying.

www.learn.columbia.edu/beauvais_imap/imap.html#
Take a look around Beauvais Cathedral with the help of the interactive map on this website.

www.sptimes.com/News/050700/TampaBay/Horrific_accident_ cre.shtml
Find out more about the collapse of the Sunshine Skyway Bridge, including first-person accounts of the events that day.

Further research

There have been many building failures and structural collapses in addition to the ones mentioned in this book. You could research some of the following:

- The Kobe earthquake, Japan (1995)
- The collapse of the South Fork Dam, in Pennsylvania (1852)
- The nuclear disasters at Three Mile Island, in Pennsylvania (1979) and Chernobyl, Ukraine (1986)
- The failures of the levees protecting New Orleans, Louisiana, during Hurricane Katrina (2005)
- The collapse of the Interstate 35W Bridge in Minneapolis, Minnesota (2007)
- The Haiti earthquake (2010)

Index